ATTENTION: ORGANIZATIONS AND CORPORATIONS
Island Entertainment Media Books may be purchased for educational, business, or sales promotional use. For information, please e-mail the Special Markets Dept. at service@iemTexas.com

A Proverb a Day

Mike Smith

IEM TEXAS

Island Entertainment Media

IEM Texas

1001 N. Travis
Sherman, TX 75090

Copyright © 2016 by Mike Smith

ISBN-10:0-9974658-1-6
ISBN-13:978-0-9974658-1-5

Printed in the United States of America

Visit Island Entertainment Media on the World Wide Web at
www.iemTexas.com

Contents

Dedication

James O. Springer, my father-in-law, attended the November 26, 2016, Thanksgiving family reunion. He enjoyed Susan's cornbread dressing and the traditional Greenberg smoked turkey. When Susan asked if he wanted the chocolate sheet cake or pecan pie, he quickly replied, "yes," meaning he wanted both. He participated in the family activities as one by one family members shared thoughts about things for which they were thankful. We signed Christmas cards to send to a missionary friend. We also shared our funny jokes. Two months later on January 28, 2015, James died. This devotional book is about wisdom. James was one of the wisest men I've ever known. In honor of James, I've included, at the back of the book, his obituary and the eulogy I delivered at his funeral on Sunday, January 31, 2016.

A Proverb a Day

Mike Smith

Introduction

The purpose of *A Proverb a Day* is to provide a guide for daily devotional time. As a young Christian, I was challenged to read daily a chapter from Proverbs, a wisdom book given primarily from father to son. I was to read the chapter in Proverbs that corresponded with the day of the month. Thus, if today were June 17, I was to read Proverbs 17, and so forth.

I believe we are in a daily spiritual warfare with Satan. We need the Word of God to arm us against Satan's attacks. We need serious reflection; we need specific prayers, and yes, we need a laugh every day to help us make it through life.

Family gatherings are usually a time of food, fun, and frank advice. At our Thanksgiving gathering on November 26, 2015, we participated in three family activities:

1. One by one, we shared something for which we were thankful.
2. One by one, we wrote greetings on Christmas cards and mailed them to a missionary; this missionary could use these greeting cards as a conversation piece to share the gospel.
3. One by one, we shared our favorite "question-and-answer" or corny joke. Thus, these jokes represent the "Punnies" in this book. To say the least, these jokes are not original. Many of these jokes can be found in print from *Barbour's Great Joke Encyclopedia.* As for other jokes, the authors wish to remain anonymous.

My prayer is that *A Proverb a Day* encourages you to have a daily devotional time with God. I have organized each daily devotional time in the following manner.

1. Proverb a day—Read the Proverb that corresponds to the day of the month. The book has thirty-one chapters, so read a chapter a day that corresponds with the day of the month.
2. Pray praises and petitions to God.

11

3. Personally reflect upon the Word of God.
4. Prepare to laugh (or groan) each day with the Punnies.
5. Plan to share what you learned and what you laughed at with someone today.

Unless otherwise noted, Scriptures quoted are from the King James Version of the Bible.

Mike Smith

Proverbs 1
Wisdom

Jacksonville College where I serve as president and religion instructor is a small liberal arts college in Jacksonville, Texas. The college has been in existence since its founding in 1899. Take a moment to consider its mission statement: "Jacksonville College exists to provide a quality education from a biblical worldview that challenges minds, transforms lives, and equips students for servant leadership and lifelong learning." Notice the phrase "lifelong learning." A wise person never stops learning. A person may grow tired of classes, papers, and tests, but learning must be a lifelong avocation and pursuit.

Passage
Read Proverbs Chapter 1.

Wisdom is more than acquiring facts and information. The words "wise" and "wisdom" are used at least 125 times in Proverbs. What is wisdom? I attended a conference in my youth and heard the speaker say, "Wisdom is seeing life from God's point of view." In the world and culture of today, everyone has his or her own point of view, opinion, thoughts, and advice. On the other hand, biblical wisdom is respecting God and the truth and authority of His Word. Wisdom is seeking what God has to say on each issue and question in life.

As you read through the book of Proverbs, seek to learn and listen to what God is saying. In every religion survey class I teach, I tell my students that they need to be able to answer five basic questions about every book of the Bible: who, what, when, where, and why. For Proverbs, the answers are:

Who?   Proverbs 1:1 says, "The proverbs of Solomon, the son of David, king of Israel…" Solomon wrote most of Proverbs, but others might have contributed.

What?   Proverbs is part of the wisdom literature in the Bible. Proverbs is from the Hebrew word *mashal*, and the basic meaning is "a comparison." Much of Proverbs is a comparison or contrast of the world's view and God's point of view.

When?   Solomon wrote three books of the Bible. In 970 B.C. as a young man in love, he wrote Song of Solomon. In 950 B.C.

as a middle-aged man seeking truth, he wrote Proverbs. In 930 B. C. as an old man sharing his experiences, he wrote Ecclesiastes.

Where?   Solomon lived in and wrote from Jerusalem.

Why?   The major theme is wisdom. The whole book can be outlined as:
Proverbs 1-9: Call for wisdom
Proverbs 10-22: Contrast of wisdom
Proverbs 23-31: Counsel by wisdom

Prayer
"God, help me be still and listen to You today."

Personal Reflection
Determine to set aside 15 minutes every day to be still and read a chapter of Proverbs that corresponds to that day of the month. Be still, and let God's wisdom guide you.

"Punny"
Q: Why did the chicken cross the road?
A: He wanted to take a road trip.

Favorites of James Owen Springer (father-in-law of the author)
Born December 7, 1920

Plan to Share Today
Plan to share what you learned and what you laughed at with someone today.

Proverbs 2
Knowledge

Passage

Read Proverbs Chapter 2.

If you have ever been lost, taken the wrong road, or struggled over a decision, then you will see the value of Proverbs 2.

Knowledge is powerful. Coaches make millions of dollars for their knowledge of the game. Fortune 500 companies hire the graduates with the most knowledge in their fields. People with knowledge go places. People without knowledge don't know what to do or where to go. I do not believe everyone is required to be a college graduate in order to make a living for his or her family or to contribute to society. College is not for everyone. Many capable men and women have never completed college; yet, in today's society, the statistics seem to indicate that the more education a person has the more earning potential he or she will have.

In Proverbs, the words "path" and "way" are used 100 times. Proverbs 2 was written from the perspective of a loving father telling his son to take the right path in life. How do you stay on the right road of life? Walk with God (Proverbs 2:9). Notice the imperatives in these verses that tell us how to walk with God.

Seek—Read God's Word (verses 1, 2, 4).

Secure—Listen and memorize God's Word (verses 1-4).

Share—Apply God's Word (verse 2).

Solomon is saying in these verses that "if" you receive God's Word, obtain knowledge, and obey God's Word, then you will have knowledge to make wise decisions. This knowledge will protect you from the evils of the world.

Life is full of sad stories about promising young people who took the wrong path, and their lives were one wreck after another. What a waste. Seek God, and obtain knowledge in order to go the right way.

Prayer

"God, I ask You to guide me to the truth of Your Word. I desire to know You and Your Word."

Personal Reflection

Each day as you read God's Word, listen to God and write down one thing to learn. Writing down what God wants you to learn will help you grow in knowledge.

"Punny"

Q: What is a woodpecker's favorite kind of joke?
A: A knock-knock joke

Favorite of James Owen Springer (father-in-law of author)
Born December 7, 1920

Plan to Share Today

Plan to share what you learned and what you laughed at with someone today.

Proverbs 3
Trust

Passage
Read Proverbs 3.

Proverbs 3:5-6, "Trust in the Lord with all thine heart; and lean not unto thine own understanding. In all thy ways acknowledge him, and he shall direct thy paths."

Between Rusk and Palestine, in the deep piney woods of East Texas, is a scenic, steam engine railway route. Tourists make plans and secure tickets in advance to ride on this attraction. In the spring, the train stops halfway between Rusk and Palestine for a giant Easter egg hunt. In the summer, the Lone Ranger rescues the passengers from train robbers. At Christmastime, passengers can come in pajamas and ride the Polar Express.

Halfway along the scenic route is a bridge. The story is told that on the train's first trip, the builder of the bridge was on board the train. As the train approached the bridge, he began to question if the bridge would support the weight of the train. If it did not, then all the passengers on board would perish. The internal struggle was too much for him. Just as the train started across the bridge, he jumped to his death. He did not trust his own work; however, the bridge held up and is still in use to this day.

Trust is a critical component in all relationships. In your relationship with God, trust is essential because trust questions and reveals what you believe about God. Do you really believe He is who He says He is? Will He do what He says He will do? God expects you to trust Him, and He expects your trust to grow in Him.

Trust is also a choice. In every crucible of life, do you rely on what you think, feel, and understand, or do you simply trust God? Trust gives evidence that you acknowledge there is a God (Phillips vol.1, 78).

The hymn writer John H. Sammis said it right:

> "Trust and obey, for there's no other way
> To be happy in Jesus, but to trust and obey."

Prayer
"Lord, help me today not to go my way but to follow You."

17

Personal Reflection
Take a sheet of paper and make three columns. Label the first column "decisions." Label the second column "my way." Label the third column "God's way." In the "decisions" column, write down three decisions you are facing. List the results that would come from making the decision "my way," and list the results that would come from making the decision "God's way." Next, compare the results. Finally, make it personal. Voice which way you are going to choose.

"Punnies"
Q: What is another name for a bunch of bees?
A: A good report card

Q: What do you call a new bee?
A: A babe-bee

Favorites of L.C. Smith (father of author)
Born October 29, 1930

Plan to Share Today
Plan to share what you learned and what you laughed at with someone today.

Proverbs 4
Obey

Passage

Read Proverbs 4.

Proverbs 4 begins with an appeal to obey and ends with an application to obey.

<u>Appeal to Obey</u>: "For I give you good doctrine, forsake ye not my law" (verse 2). Solomon says his father taught him; now, Solomon wants to teach you (verses 3-4) the following benefits of obedience:

1. Protection (verse 6)
    Solomon says to love wisdom, to seek to know what God says, and to obey His Word. The result is protection.

2. Principle (verse 7)
    Solomon is trying to show the importance of wisdom. Once you know God's Word, it will guide you in every decision of life, for example, what school to attend, what occupation to pursue, whom to marry, and where to live.

<u>Application of Obeying</u>: Solomon closes this proverb with a physical application about how to obey. In verses 23-27 he uses various body parts to remind us how to apply wisdom.

1. Heart (verse 23)
    The heart is the source of all actions. Your heart must be right if life is to be right.

2. Mouth (verse 24)
    A person's words can get him or her into trouble.

3. Eyes (verse 25)
    Much temptation begins with the eye. Every year at Jacksonville College, I appeal to students in the area of dress. Men are aroused by a "look." Provocative dress appeals to the flesh. Satan's appeal to Eve in the garden was through a "look" at the forbidden fruit.

4. Feet (verses 26-27)
    Be careful where you go. If you avoid bars or places where alcohol is served, chances are good that you won't get drunk.

Prayer

"God, guide my heart, mouth, eyes, and feet today so that I will obey You."

Personal Reflection

Read God's Word to start your day so that you have power and protection as you walk.

"Punny"

Q: What do you call a bear with no teeth?
A: A gummy bear

Favorite of L.C. Smith (father of author)
Born October 29, 1930

Plan to Share Today

Plan to share what you learned and what you laughed at with someone today.

Proverbs 5
Sex

Passage

Read Proverbs 5.

The dominant theme of Proverbs 5 is sex. The dominant theme of the world is sex. It seems that almost every song played, every show aired, and every commercial displayed is full of suggestive, sexual overtones. I saw a commercial recently where a couple in their 80s who were sitting at the breakfast table. The sponsor portrayed eating breakfast cereal as a way to improve your sex life. Some commercials are all about sex and have only one scene at the end to show the product they are really selling. Every perversion of sex seems to be accepted by society. For this reason, fathers need to have conversations with their sons about sex. Even though these conversations may be awkward, a father cannot afford to neglect this responsibility. While this chapter was written from a masculine perspective, the message applies to women as well. Mothers need to have discussions about sex with their daughters. Proverbs gives a good outline for this talk.

Counsel Against Adultery (verses 1-4)

> Adultery is used to depict any sex outside of the bonds of marriage (Exodus 20:14; Leviticus 20:10; Proverbs 2:16-19; 6:20-35; 7:1-27). The terms used in these verses, "loose woman," "neighbor's wife," "strange woman," and "foreign woman" all refer to sex outside of marriage. Sex outside of marriage is appealing, but in reality, it is as destructive as a two-edged sword.

Consequences of Adultery (verses 4-23)

1. Leaves a bitter memory and guilt (verse 4)
2. Leads to hell (verse 5)
3. Destroys your health (verse 9)
4. Robs you financially (Affairs are expensive.) (verse 10)
5. Disgraces the church (verse 14)
6. Robs you of great sex with your spouse (verses 15-20)
7. Does not escape God's knowledge (verse 21)
8. Separates you from God (verses 22-23)

Prayer

"God, keep my eyes on Jesus. Keep me obedient to my covenant with my spouse. Give me strength to say 'no' to temptation."

Personal Reflection

Talk with your sons and daughters before it's too late. Talk with your spouse, and let her or him satisfy you because that is God's design and is the best way.

"Punnies"

Q: What excuse did Adam give to his children as to why he no longer lived in the Garden of Eden?
A: "Your mother ate us out of house and home."

Q: What do people have today that Adam didn't have?
A: Ancestors

Favorites of Dot Smith (mother of author)
Born March 6, 1933

Plan to Share Today

Plan to share what you learned and what you laughed at with someone today.

Proverbs 6
God's Hate List

Passage
Read Proverbs 6.

People have used lists for centuries. Mothers make grocery lists; comedians have their "Top Ten" lists, and the FBI has their "Most Wanted" lists. God has His list of seven things He hates beginning in Proverbs 6:16-19. The church often refers to this list as the "Seven Deadly Sins."

Verse 16 is an idiomatic Hebrew expression and implies that there are more than just seven deadly sins, but seven will be dealt with here. The seven deadly sins are characteristics of Lucifer. Jesus is the contrast. The first five deadly sins refer to body parts, and the last two refer to bad people.

1. Pride/Proud Look/Eyes (verse 17)
   This person is arrogant and refuses to trust God. This sin describes the attitude of the heart.

2. Lies/Lying Tongue (verse 17)
   This person has no regard or value for the truth and will distort reality. This sin often leads to psychopathic personality disorders.

3. Anger/Hands (verse 17)
   This person lacks self-control and will often act violently with his hands before thinking.

4. Envy/Heart (verse 18)
   This person devises wicked schemes and has no regard for right or wrong. This person is selfish and will do anything to get his or her way. This is a sociopathic person.

5. Greed/Feet (verse 18)
   This person wants something for nothing and is quick to do wrong.

6. False Witness/Person Who Lies (verse 19)
   This person lies, even in court, with no regard for truth, justice, and order in society. He or she cares only about himself or herself and not for others.

7. Sows Discord/Person Who Causes Conflict (verse 19)

This person gossips, lies, stirs up trouble, and causes conflict with no regard to what he or she does to other people. This behavior often breaks up relationships, whether they be with spouses, with family, with friends, or with the church.

Prayer
"God, help me to avoid these seven deadly sins today. Help me to be more like Jesus."

Personal Reflection
Take notes throughout the day. At the end of the day, list the number of seven deadly sins you observed. Did you display a sin for which you need to repent?

"Punny"
Q: What time of day was Adam created?
A: Just before Eve

Favorite of Dot Smith (mother of author)
Born March 6, 1933

Plan to Share Today
Plan to share what you learned and what you laughed at with someone today.

Proverbs 7
Bad Company Pollutes Good Character

Passage

Read Proverbs 7.

Involved parents need to be concerned about who their children's friends are. Proverbs 7 is a scene with a father who warns his son about "hanging out" with bad company. This father tells a story of looking out a window and watching a man being led astray.

Notice the means by which the woman portrayed in this proverb leads the man astray.

1. Prostitute clothing (verse 10)
   A man is tempted and aroused by sight.

2. Pursuit (verses 11-12)
   The woman is the pursuer instead of the man. She is the aggressor and reverses the role. Weak men are vulnerable to this behavior.

3. Physical touch (verse 13)
   The woman kisses him. Sensual kisses or touches weaken a man's defense.

4. Peace (verse 14)
   One interpretation of this verse is that the woman tries to justify the sin by saying, "I have been to the temple and made my offering, so now let's have some fun." She believes the lie that being religious on Sunday is rewarded with having fun on Saturday. The other interpretation is that the woman is a prostitute in a cult temple and that she needs to pay her vow.

5. Pleasing words (verses 15-16)
   Erotic language is stimulating and seductive.

6. Perfume (verse 17)
   The senses are aroused by smell.

7. Provided opportunity (verses 18-20)
   The woman continues to justify sin.

Sadly, good men with full lives are led astray and destroy their lives for just a few moments of physical pleasure. What a high price to pay.

Prayer
"God, help me to carefully choose my friends and the places where I go."

Personal Reflection
How could the man have avoided and how can I avoid this sexual snare?

"Punnies"
Q: What kind of music do steelworkers listen to?
A: Heavy metal

Q: What do you call a lazy doctor?
A: Dr. Doolittle

Favorites of Carol Elaine Springer Chambers (sister-in-law of author)
Born July 24, 1946

Plan to Share Today
Plan to share what you learned and what you laughed at with someone today.

Proverbs 8
Creator

Passage

Read Proverbs 8.

Part of the mission statement at Jacksonville College is "to provide a quality education from a biblical worldview." Thus, our science teachers are creationists. They teach as the Bible presents the truth that God is Creator. The world teaches from an evolutionist's perspective. This worldview is one of chaos, randomness, and accidents. Some scientists use the "Big Bang" theory to explain the existence of our world.

The biblical worldview is the Genesis account that "In the beginning, God created the heaven and the earth." The world is a masterpiece of design, beauty, function, and wisdom. An honest observation of the world leads to the conclusion that an intelligent designer created this marvel.

The word "possessed" in Proverbs 8:22 in the King James Version of the Bible in the Septuagint (the Greek translation of the Old Testament) means "created." The teaching that God is Creator annoys and irritates some scientists. However, all of creation is the stage on which God displays His wisdom. Look at how God is Creator:

1. Sea (verse 24)
    Of the 197 million square miles of the earth's surface, 145 million square miles are below the sea. God created this ratio. Without this perfect ratio, the temperature and seasons would change disastrously (Phillips vol. 1, 200).

2. Stars (verses 27-28)
    The naked eye can see about seven thousand stars. Just in our galaxy alone, the Milky Way, there are said to be over one hundred billion stars. These stars, the moon, the sun, and the earth are all in motion. The moon revolves around the earth, the earth around the sun, and the sun around the galaxy—all functioning at precise speeds and distances. If the earth rotated any faster, we would fly off the earth; if the earth spun any slower, we would freeze to death. If the earth were any closer to the sun, we would burn up (Phillips vol. 1, 205).

Because God is Creator, He is sovereign. God is on His throne and controls all things. This truth should motivate us to serve Him.

Prayer
"God, I bow before You as Creator. There is none like You, and beside You, there is no other. Thank You for a beautiful world."

Personal Reflection
Just as God has a plan for everything He created, He has a plan for you and me. Think back on how God has worked in your life, and write it down. Be in awe of His creation.

"Punny"
Q: Why did the cabbage win the race?
A: It was ahead.

Favorite of Carol Elaine Springer Chambers (sister-in-law of author)
Born July 24, 1946

Plan to Share Today
Plan to share what you learned and what you laughed at with someone today.

Proverbs 9
Fear of the Lord

Passage
Read Proverbs 9.

Proverbs 9:10 says, "The fear of the Lord is the beginning of wisdom." The fear of the Lord is to stand in awe and to be filled with reverence and respect for who God is. I tell my students that when the scribes were copying the Scripture and they came to the name of God, they would lay down their pens, go wash and change clothes, and come back to write "God." When they came to God's name again, they repeated the ritual. While this ritual may seem silly and ridiculous, it revealed a high reverence and respect for God.

Today, respect for anyone is rarely seen. Too many people treat everyone and everything as "common." In times past, parents would correct their children by saying, "Don't run in church! Be quiet in God's house!" When a preacher visited someone and that person was drinking beer, he or she would hide the beer out of respect for a man of God. Today, that person would probably offer the preacher a can and continue to drink.

In the 1700s, Jonathan Edwards read a sermon called "Sinners in the Hands of an Angry God." As he read, people literally fell out in the aisles, crying and weeping out of fear of God. Not so today. People have seen so many shootings and bombings on the daily news and entertainment shows that they are desensitized to the horrors of hell and fear of God.

Fear of the Lord or respect or reverence for who He is will lead you to treat the things of God differently. You will believe the Bible is God's inspired, inerrant, infallible Word and seek to know it. You will take time to worship God daily, not seasonally. You will give tithes, not out of duty but out of love and devotion as a trust in who God is. You will go to church to fellowship with God's people and express love to God. You will serve the hungry and show God's love to others.

Prayer
"God, You are holy, and beside You, there is no other. I bow in love and respect."

Personal Reflection
List ways in which you can express the fear of God today.

"Punnies"
Q: Why did the doughnut-maker retire?
A: He was fed up with the hole business.

Q: Why don't matches play baseball?
A: One strike and they're out.

Favorites of Edmond Mason Rollins (nephew of author)
Born October 30, 1968

Plan to Share Today
Share an attribute of God today with someone. When someone disrespects
God by using His name as a curse word, express your respect for God.

Proverbs 10
Work

Passage
Read Proverbs 10.

Proverbs 10:5, 26, "He that gathereth in summer is a wise son: but he that sleepeth in harvest is a son that causeth shame . . . As vinegar to the teeth, and as smoke to the eyes, so is the sluggard to them that send him."

I am thankful that my parents instilled in me a strong work ethic. My dad left the logging business of Alabama for the oilfields of Texas. He started at the bottom and worked hard. At one time, he was the largest independent oilfield contractor in Texas with over 200 vehicles for which he had to buy tags. My mother, like my dad, never finished high school. She put herself through beautician school and opened a beauty shop. Later, she opened an antique shop, and in her later life, she was a designer and manufacturer of children's clothing.

My parents achieved success because they worked. My dad used to tell me, "Do something. Even if it is wrong, just do something." My parents had very little patience or sympathy for lazy people. They passed this trait on to me. I've seen lazy workers who are always looking for more money and less work. I've witnessed lazy students who procrastinate until the deadline passes. They lose their scholarships and are placed on academic probation; some students are dismissed from the college.

A "sluggard" in the King James Version is a lazy person, for example, someone who procrastinates and tries to avoid work. The comedian W.C. Fields said, "The laziest man I ever met put popcorn in his pancakes so they would turn over by themselves."

Verses 5 and 26 urge against laziness and procrastination. People in East Texas say, "Make hay while the sun shines." Verse 26 expresses the irritation and the disdain a lazy person causes. Value work, and thank God for the opportunity and health to work.

Prayer
"God, thank You for giving to me the opportunity, health, and skill to work."

Personal Reflection
List jobs you have had and how God used them to teach you. List your dream job and what it takes to achieve it.

"Punny"
Q: What animal has more lives than a cat?
A: A frog, because he croaks every night.

Favorite of Edmond Mason Rollins (nephew of author)
Born October 30, 1968

Plan to Share Today
Plan to share what you learned and what you laughed at with someone today.

Proverbs 11
Counsel

Passage
Read Proverbs 11.

Proverbs 11:14 says, "Where no counsel is, the people fall: but in the multitude of counsellors there is safety." The word "counsel" in this verse means "helmsman." A helmsman is a guide or a person who sets the direction of a ship. Relying on your own wisdom when making decisions in life is dangerous. You need other people. Who are some people from whom you should seek advice when facing an issue?

1. Parents
   Proverbs is filled with verses about listening to our parents. You never get too old to listen to your parents, but an eroding factor in current society is the absence of parents who are godly. Sadly, many youth today are without a spiritual leader or role model in their homes.

2. Pastor
   As a believer, you should be active in a local church where you can feel comfortable going to your pastor and asking for advice and prayer. In turn, every pastor should have compassion and concern for his members whom he takes the time to counsel. Pastors need to be spiritual leaders who, from the pulpit, give answers to life's questions from a biblical view.

3. Personal friends
   Proverbs 27:9 says, "Ointment and perfume rejoice the heart: so doth the sweetness of a man's friend by hearty counsel." Proverbs 27:17 says, "Iron sharpeneth iron; so a man sharpeneth the countenance of his friend." Not every friend is a good source from whom to seek counsel. I do not advocate running from person to person and seeking advice because this will be confusing. Be careful. Select friends who will pray for you and speak truth in love.

During my years of working with pastors, those who got into trouble and failed in their ministry were "Lone Ranger" Christians who thought they did not need another person's counsel. During my entire ministry, I've sought out and made friends. Usually, this happens at Dairy Queen or Whataburger around 10:00 a.m. while I'm enjoying a cup of coffee. Weekly, I've tried to be a part of a men's accountability group. If you develop this type of relationship, you can't fool these friends or mask your feelings when you are around them; they will know you are troubled and try to help you.

Prayer
"God, thank You for friends. I thank You for bringing
_____ into my life."

(names of friends)

Personal Reflection
Make friends. "A man that hath friends must shew himself friendly" (Proverbs 18:24). Take your friend out to lunch this week. Tell your friend "thank you."

"Punnies"
Q: How does the Easter bunny stay fit?
A: He eggs-ercises and does hare-robics.

Q: Why did the Easter egg hide?
A: He was a little chicken.

Favorites of Susan Claire Springer Smith (wife of author)
Born May 21, 1950

Plan to Share Today
Plan to share what you learned and what you laughed at with someone today.

Proverbs 12
Words

Passage

Read Proverbs 12.

Do you recall the childhood nursery rhyme about words?

"Sticks and stones may break my bones
But words will never hurt me."

This phrase is not true because words can and do hurt. Solomon teaches that words can bring about two results:

1. Words can bring war.
    Verse 17—A false witness [utters] deceit.
    Verse 18—[One] speaketh like the piercings of a sword.
    Verse 22—Lying lips are [an] abomination to the Lord.

    Words are powerful weapons. Some people use words like a warrior uses a sword to cut down his enemies. People who use words to cut down another person intend to hurt that person. Sometimes this act of wounding with words is used to get revenge.

    Lies are an abomination to the Lord. Lies usually hurt someone. As a young boy, I told a lie, and it hurt a relationship between two family members. I still regret it to this day.

2. Words can bring peace.
    Verse 17—Truth sheweth forth righteousness.
    Verse 18—The tongue of the wise is health.
    Verse 19—The lip of truth shall be established for ever.
    Verse 20—Counsellors of peace [have] joy.
    Verse 21—[Protection comes] to the just.

    Good words, kind words, and profound words give peace. The right words can defuse the tensest situation. Right words can provide protection against the enemy. Jesus used the Word of God to resist the devil. You need to have an arsenal of Bible verses to speak truth and defuse the enemy.

Prayer

"God, guard my tongue today. Lord, may I praise You and bring peace to others with my words."

Personal Reflection

Make a point today to say a kind word to five people.

"Punnies"

Q: Why did the strawberry need a lawyer?
A: It was in a jam.

Q: What kind of fish do you use to make a peanut butter sandwich?
A: A jellyfish

Favorites of William Mike Smith (author)
Born June 17, 1950

Plan to Share Today

Plan to share what you learned and what you laughed at with someone today.

Proverbs 13
Family

Passage

Read Proverbs 13.

I thank God for my family. A couple of times a year, I really get interested in genealogy. I update my subscription to Ancestry.com, and I read my family tree. As a believer in the sovereignty of God, I realize that I could have been born in Africa, Poland, or Spain. I also realize that I could have been born into a family of criminals, atheists, and harlots. However, I was born a Smith to L.C. and Dot Smith in the rural South. I have certain values and benefits because of my family.

Solomon speaks of family. What should a person pass on to the next generation?

1. Legacy
    Verse 22 says, "A good man leaveth an inheritance to his children's children: and the wealth of the sinner is laid up for the just." The world thinks about "How much will my inheritance be?" There is more to legacy than money. What about a good name? I am a Smith. Now some people think of "Smith" as dull. I was told that everyone was a Smith, but when they started sinning, cheating, and lying, they changed their names to Brown, Jones, or some other name.

    I am thankful for my family tree. My mother's parents were William Curtis and Annie Carr Davis. They were hard-working farmers in East Mississippi. My dad's parents were Wilburn and Helen Downey Smith. He was a logger who worked hard and built a good company. My dad and mother never finished high school, but my dad worked hard. He worked his way up until he owned a large oil company with a good name in Texas. My mother was a beautician, antique store owner, and designer of children's clothing. I thank God for my legacy.

2. Labor
    Verse 23 says, "Much food is in the tillage of the poor: but there is that is destroyed for want of judgment." A major part of my legacy is my labor or work ethic. I know of no lazy Smiths; the lazy ones are the ones who changed their names.

3. Love

Verse 24 says, "He that spareth his rod hateth his son: but he that loveth him chasteneth him betimes." My dad whipped me only twice. He had a look and a way of correcting that hurt much more than any rod. Both of my parents gave me much freedom and trust, but they disciplined me early in life and instilled right in me.

Prayer
"God, I thank You for my family."

Personal Reflection
Write out your family history, and share it with someone.

"Punny"
Q: Why do chickens like thunderstorms?
A: They enjoy fowl weather.

Favorites of William James Gardner (son-in-law of author)
Born September 20, 1970

Plan to Share Today
Plan to share what you learned and what you laughed at with someone today.

Proverbs 14
Backslider

Passage

Read Proverbs 14.

Proverbs 14:14, "The backslider in heart shall be filled with his own ways: and a good man shall be satisfied from himself."

During the first eleven years of my life, I lived in the city of Houston. I could walk to the end of my street and get a Coke and candy at Chinaman's Store. On Saturdays, I could walk to the movie theater, see a movie for a quarter, buy a Coke for a nickel, and get a bag of popcorn for ten cents. Then, I could watch Roy Rogers for two hours. Afterwards, I could walk to the drug store and get a chocolate malt.

One day, without any family discussion, without any vote or research of alternatives, my dad announced that we were moving to Raccoon Bend. My life suddenly changed. It really wasn't bad. I just had many new experiences. I have one memory of when I entered the county fair calf scramble. Seventy-five boys lined up on one end of the arena, and 20 calves were on the other end. I was not fast then, or now, so, as the other boys raced down to catch a calf, I steadily moved along the fence. A white-faced heifer made her way towards me. I caught her and put my halter on her face. However, as I pulled her towards the finish, she resisted and backed up in the opposite direction. She finally slid backwards, sat down, and sang "I shall not be moved."

This was my first experience with a backsliding heifer. Later, in reading the Bible, I discovered that the term "backslider" is used sixteen times to describe people. While not everyone agrees on the meaning of the term "backslider," consider the following three views:

1. Arminian view—Backsliding is the process of actually falling from grace, and a person loses his or her salvation.
2. Calvinist view—A backslider is a person who is still saved but has lost fellowship with God.
3. Pentecostal view—A backslider is a person who has never been saved.

Proverbs 14:14 says, "[A] backslider in his heart shall be filled with his own ways." Backsliding is going against or away from the direction in which God intends for you to go.

Prayer

"God, help me to walk with You and not away from You."

Personal Reflection

Do a personal reflection. Are your heart and lifestyle moving with God or away from God?

"Punny"

Q: What's the difference between the government and the Mafia?
A: Only one of them is organized.

Favorite of William James Gardner (son-in-law of author)
Born September 20, 1970

Plan to Share Today

Plan to share what you learned and what you laughed at with someone today.

Proverbs 15
Answer

Passage
Read Proverbs 15.

Do you ever notice how people respond when you phone them? For over twenty years, my wife, Susan, was the secretary in offices for associations of Baptist churches. Pastors and lay people often commented on the pleasant telephone voice that she had. Her answer was often, "Hello, Dogwood Trails Baptist Area, this is Susan; how may I help you?" You can phone some people and the only answers you receive are "Hey," "Uh," or "Yeah." Sometimes you can tell that people are angry when you call because their reply is, "What do you want?" I've had some friends who answer their phone calls with ridiculous statements such as "Joe's Mule Barn, feed fifty cents," or "Bill's Fix-it Shop, what do you need to straighten out?"

In working for over forty years with church secretaries, Baptist association secretaries, convention receptionists, business receptionists, and individuals, I have heard people answer callers with varying words and tones. My Susan was the best.

How you answer a person, whether it be via phone or in person, can make all the difference in the remaining direction of the conversation. Proverbs gives us some help on how to answer.

1. Soft answer (verse 1)
    When someone is rude, crude, loud, and mean in his or her conversation to you, how do you respond? Most people want to reply in a ruder, cruder, and louder voice to get that person's attention. The Bible says, "A soft answer turneth away wrath." How true. When people are loud, but you respond with a soft whisper, it disarms them.

2. Straight answer (verses 2-3)
    You must know what you are talking about. You must be *accurate* in what you say (verse 2) because you will be held *accountable* for what you say (verse 3). Have you ever had a talk with someone and at the end of the conversation said to yourself, "He did not know what he was talking about"?

3. Sweet answer (verse 4)

The right answer, a sweet answer, is so encouraging. I can be down in the dumps, depressed, or hurt by others' words, and God sends someone who says, "Bro. Mike, you are such a help." I perk up and am encouraged. My grandmother said, "You can catch more bees with honey than with vinegar."

Prayer
"Lord, help me guard my answers; let them be helpful and not hurtful.

Personal Reflection
When you receive an email, don't respond in all caps—that is shouting. Stop, pray, think, and respond with kindness.

"Punny"
Q: Who was the first tennis player in the Bible?
A: Joseph—he served in Pharaoh's court.

Favorite of Martha Elaine Smith Gardner (daughter of author)
Born December 2, 1974

Plan to Share Today
Plan to share what you learned and what you laughed at with someone today.

Proverbs 16
Old Age

Read Proverbs 16.

Proverbs 16:31, "The hoary head is a crown of glory, if it be found in the way of righteousness."

Some people fear growing old. History records people who gave their lives in search of the "fountain of youth." Today, the latest "anti-wrinkle cream" is a best seller. To those people I say, "Getting old has its problems, but it beats the alternative of dying young." I am in that group of "hoary heads" (white or gray headed). What little hair I have is a mix of white and gray. Actually, I have always enjoyed being around "old people."

My grandparents were fun people, especially Granddaddy Davis and Grandmother Smith. My fondest memories as a child are of sitting in front of the fireplace at Granddaddy Davis's feet and listening as he entertained us with stories; he was a master storyteller. Most of his stories ended with a loud, hearty laugh. My Grandmother Smith, on the other hand, was full of advice and had remedies for every ailment. I remember as a young boy "breaking wind" or "passing gas" in her presence, and she was quick to advise me to take antacid. She further reminded me that "gas kills more people than any other ailment." I quickly countered, "Grandmother, that's crazy; gas doesn't kill people." Later, when I got older, I had gallbladder surgery. As is characteristic with this type of surgery, my stomach was full of gas. Those gas pains nearly killed me. I whispered, "Grandmother, you were right."

Much of my ministry in church has been blessed by old, "hoary heads." I remember a group of older women who would meet and pray for our youth group at First Baptist Church in Bellville, Texas. When I was a very young and inexperienced nineteen-year-old, it was a small group of old people who called me to be their pastor. Over the years, I have spoken to senior adult groups such as Golden Jubilee, Young at Heart, and others. I have noticed two different tactics some people take towards getting old:

1. Some fight it.
   Some people exercise, eat right, dress young, and do everything in their power not to grow or look old. Others go to extremes in youthful dressing, plastic surgery, and "washing away the gray" in hopes of camouflaging the signs of aging.

2. Some "faith" it.
   Some people grow old gracefully; they continue to serve the Lord. They realize they cannot do what they used to do, but they keep serving. One great example is The Master's Builders, a group of retired men and women in the Baptist Missionary Association, who give their time to build churches. During my tenure as President of Jacksonville College, they have built or refurbished some building on our campus every summer.

Prayer
"God, help me not to grow old and bitter; I want to grow old with grace."

Personal Reflection
Plan for your future. Are you prepared for old age? It will come quickly.

"Punny"
Q: Why is Christmas like a day at the office?
A: Because you do all the work, and the fat guy in the suit gets all the credit.

Favorite of Martha Elaine Smith Gardner (daughter of author)
Born December 2, 1974

Plan to Share Today
Plan to share what you learned and what you laughed at with someone today.

Proverbs 17
Grandchildren

Passage
Read Proverbs 17

Take a look at verse 6: "Children's children are the crown of old men; and the glory of children are their fathers." This verse is a beautiful picture of an old grandfather delighting in his family. Many people in American culture do not value the family. Consider some of the current terms in use: "shacking up," "common-law marriages," "significant others," "office wives," "no-fault divorce," and "latch-key children."

Seeing a family together is a beautiful sight. I recently preached a revival for a church whose young pastor and family encouraged and blessed me. Every night, the pastor's wife and their four, cleanly and neatly dressed, very polite children filled a pew. I got more out of their witness each evening than I did the sermon I was preaching.

I also thank God for my grandchildren. Do you want to see my pictures? Martha and James have blessed me with three grandchildren, and Lance and Ashley have blessed me with two. William is the oldest grandchild. When he was two years old and would come to visit us, he would reach up and grab my fingers because he wanted to walk around the block. I enjoyed those walks, but the greatest walk I had with him was on Saturday before he was baptized. Susan and I had traveled to witness his baptism, and as soon as I arrived, he didn't have to reach up for my hand anymore, but he wanted me to join with him and walk around the block where he lived. As we walked, he stopped at every house and invited them to his baptism. My granddaughter, Emma Gardner, has really transformed into a beautiful, godly woman. When she was small, I was concerned because she didn't crawl like most children. My worries were unfounded. Today, she is a top student, plays in the marching band, is an excellent cook, and loves the Lord. Jacob, Elaine and James's youngest son, is the comedian of the family. He laughs at everything and is fun to be with. Logan Curtis Smith and Landon Cole Smith are the two sons of our son Lance Curtis Smith. Notice that their names all form the initials "L.C." My father was L.C.—no name, just the two letters. Lance wanted to use his grandfather's two letters in naming his sons. Both of Lance's sons are ball players and, along with our grandson Jacob, enjoy collecting baseball and football trading cards. Logan and Landon live near us, and we enjoy watching them play baseball or taking them to card shops. God gave us a double blessing when he gave us grandchildren.

Prayer
"God, I thank You for blessing me with grandchildren."

Personal Reflection
Write the "specialties" of each of your grandchildren, and share them with another person or a group of people. If you don't have any grandchildren, seek to be an influence in a younger life.

"Punnies"
Q: What kind of man was Boaz before he married?
A: He was Ruthless.

Q: Which man in the Bible had no parents?
A: Joshua—he was the son of Nun.

Favorites of Emily Claire "Emma" Gardner (granddaughter of author)
Born November 20, 2000

Plan to Share Today
Plan to share what you learned and what you laughed at with someone today.

Proverbs 18
Friends

Passage

Read Proverbs 18.

Proverbs 18:24, "A man that hath friends must shew himself friendly: and there is a friend that sticketh closer than a brother."

I heard a speaker say, "If you have five friends you are a fortunate man." Well I am blessed and have been very fortunate in my life to have friends. Every stage of life and in every place I have resided I have made friends that remain friends to this day. As a young boy living on the bayous of Houston, my friends and I fought dragons and played Cowboys and Indians. As a teenager living in rural Austin County, I was part of a youth group that met every Sunday evening after church to pray and play together. We did this without formal leaders. It was out of desire to want to be together. As a pastor, in every town I lived in I had a friend who would meet me at Whataburger or the Dairy Queen at ten o'clock for coffee and fellowship. Today, on Mondays I meet with a group of friends at noon for salad and meatballs and time to share and pray together. Rare is a day that a friend does not call me or I him to laugh and visit. I do believe I have friends because I made the effort to make friends.

People I witness today who live lonely and empty lives are the "Lone Ranger," type who live in an isolated world. Remember even Lone Ranger had Tonto. Yes, friends will disappoint you and may even turn on you, but they are still valuable parts of our lives. There is a friend I meet every morning before I see any other, and this friend is closer than any brother. That is my friend Jesus. Joseph M. Scriven in 1855 wrote song, "What a Friend We Have in Jesus." He wrote it to comfort his mother for they were separated by many miles. Fellowship with Jesus is a comfort, and He is a friend like no other.

Prayer

"God, help me resist the lusts of this world and learn of You. You are my strength. As the hymn 'Just as I Am' says, 'I am weak but thou art strong.'"

Personal Reflection

Ask God to reveal to you a characteristic of the world in you that you need to separate yourself from and a characteristic of Jesus that you need to seek.

"Punnies"

Q: What do you call a dog in January?
A: A chili dog

Q: What day of the week is the chicken most afraid of?
A: Fry-day

Favorites of William James Gardner (grandson of author)
Born November 18, 1998

Plan to Share Today

Plan to share what you learned and what you laughed at with someone today.

Proverbs 19
Poor

Passage
Read Proverbs 19.

In helping the poor, be careful to:

1. Never enable them to continue to be poor.
   Sometimes when you give money to someone who is poor, you enable them to stay poor. Which is better? To give a man a fish or to teach him to fish?

2. Never overlook that they are people.
   Some people respond to the sight of a poor man by not looking at him or by turning away and going the opposite direction. Some people look at the poor man but with disgust, asking "Why doesn't he get a job?" Some people look at the poor man defensively saying, "I worked hard for what I have, and I must take care of my own family."

Once I was asked to play the role of a "bum" or "poor man" in a skit at my church. We were having an emphasis on ministering to the homeless. I agreed. I did not shave; I put on torn, soiled clothes, and I spread sardines and limburger cheese on my clothes to give an offensive odor. I decided that before I went to the church program, I would first go to the local convenience store and sit on the sidewalk in a corner near the door. The owner was aware of who I was and agreed. As I sat there, these were the reactions of some of the people as they passed by me.

1. Some paid no attention and hurried about their business.
2. Some looked but just kept going.
3. Some came over and dropped money, which I later gave to the church.
4. A few came over and talked to me.

I later arrived at the church where I was to participate in the skit about ministering to the homeless. Instead of going inside, in the same way that I had sat outside of the convenience store, I sat on the sidewalk outside the doors of the church. The reactions of passers-by were really no different than those at the convenience store, except that I received more money at the convenience store than I did from the church people.

When you lend to the poor, you lend to God. Lending is sometimes in the form money, but sometimes lending involves more than money. Lending can be in the form of prayer, personal time, and presentation of the gospel.

Prayer
"God, open my eyes and heart to those who are hurting near me."

Personal Reflection

 Discover ways to help the poor. Talk to a church leader and discover a family who needs help in church.

"Punny"
Q: Why was the computer so tired when it got home from work?
A: Because it had a hard drive

Favorite of William James Gardner (grandson of author)
Born November 18, 1998

Plan to Share Today
Plan to share what you learned and what you laughed at with someone today.

Proverbs 20
Wine

Passage

Read Proverbs 20.

Proverbs 20:1, "Wine is a mocker, strong drink is raging: and whosoever is deceived thereby is not wise."

My grandfather on my mother's side drank a lot of moonshine whiskey in rural Mississippi. When he was sober, he was the kindest, funniest, most hard-working man. Life was tough in the 1930s-60s in rural Mississippi. My grandfather had to work from sunup to sunset on the red land of Mississippi to provide food for his family. He lost four children, two in child birth, one child who died of heart problems in his teenage years, and one child in the military at the start of World War II. My grandfather's life was hard but not an excuse for his behavior. Though he worked hard all week, he got drunk on the weekends. He became so addicted to alcohol that the family had to have him committed, and my grandmother moved out of the house. I've witnessed this division and these hurts of a loving family. I've seen first-hand the pain that results from strong drink.

We never had alcohol in our home. However, I had plenty of opportunities to drink. I grew up in a German/Czech community where drinking beer was the same as drinking water. Even though I had many opportunities to drink, I've always chosen not to drink for two reasons.

1. The Bible warns against drinking.
   In Proverbs 20 Solomon says that wine is a mocker and whoever drinks it is not wise. Alcoholism is a major problem in America. Some cultures might drink in moderation, but Americans—for the most part—drink to get drunk. Drunk driving is still the number one cause of traffic fatalities. Drinking destroys homes, bankrupts careers, and costs society billions of dollars. Heed these warnings. Going to heaven is not based on whether or not a person drinks alcohol. Going to heaven is based on a relationship with Jesus Christ. However, I believe it is best to heed the warnings in God's Word and refrain from drinking. Be a "teetotaler."

2. The Bible warns against harming your witness.
   You never know who is watching: a friend, a neighbor, your child, or your grandchild. Your drinking could be viewed by other

people as a big endorsement. Paul shares this wisdom in 1 Corinthians 8:9, "But take heed lest by any means this liberty of yours become a stumbling block to them that are weak." I do not want to cause anyone to stumble.

Prayer
"God, help me to refrain from drinking alcohol so that I will not influence my children, grandchildren, and others near me to drink alcohol."

Personal Reflection
Develop your own convictions. Do your own study in and with the Bible about the dangers of alcohol.

"Punny"
Q: How do you know when the grapes are old and tired?
A: They start to wine.

Favorite of William Mike Smith (author)
Born June 17, 1950

Plan to Share Today
Plan to share what you learned and what you laughed at with someone today.

Proverbs 21
Pursuits

Passage
Read Proverbs 21.

What do you want? What are you chasing? What are you seeking to find? In these verses, Solomon gives some wisdom on what not to pursue and what to pursue.

1. Negative pursuits (verse 17)
    Chasing pleasure will leave you empty. The world is full of stories about those people who seek pleasure to give meaning to life. It is staggering to observe people who work five days a week and spend all their earnings on a weekend of pleasure. Listen to some conversations, and all you hear is, "What are you going to do this weekend?" Some people pursue pleasure in sports; they will pay hundreds of dollars for a hard seat at a game and pay five times the normal price for a cold hot dog during the game. When it's all over, they waste an hour or more while sitting in the parking lot and trying to exit. Some people pursue hunting; all they live for is to rise two hours before the sun, sit in a freezing cold deer stand, and wait for a lonely, lovely creature of God to walk in front of their .270 rifles. Some people pursue wine; weekend drunks wreak havoc on the highways and ruin family life each weekend. A normal, good man who behaves well all week turns into a wild animal on the weekends. Some people pursue sex; they fantasize, flirt, and finagle until they enjoy a moment of ecstasy. Afterwards, they live with the guilt and shame.

2. Positive pursuit (verse 21)
    Jesus restated this proverb in Matthew 6:33, "But seek ye first the kingdom of God, and his righteousness; and all these things shall be added unto you." To seek righteousness is to seek that which is right in the sight of God. The idea behind mercy here is love. Righteousness speaks of law and mercy of love. A man who pursues the law and love finds life (Phillips Vol. 2, 101-2 outline).

Prayer

"God, help me to see clearly the eternal things of life. Help me to pursue You."

Personal Reflection

Before you plan a trip, write a check list, stop, and ask, "Will this honor God?"

"Punnies"

Q: Where do cows usually go on dates?
A: To the moo-vies

Q: What goes tick-tock woof-woof?
A: A watchdog

Favorites of Jacob Andrew Gardner (grandson of author)
Born May 5, 2005

Plan to Share Today

Plan to share what you learned and what you laughed at with someone today.

Proverbs 22
Education in Mind, Money, and Morals

Passage

Read Proverbs 22.

The students at Jacksonville College are primarily just out of high school and away from home for the first time. As the current president, I see many struggling as they face temptations and opportunities that were never before afforded to them. So, the administrators, teachers, and coaches try to provide not only the basic education but also advice concerning money and morals.

At JC, we have students from one extreme to the other. Some students come to us from developing countries and literally have nothing to bring with them. We picked up one young lady from the airport; she had only one bag. When she opened the bag, she discovered that her mother, who had escorted her to the airport, had taken all of the clothes out of the bag and kept them for herself. We had to purchase bedding and clothing for this young lady. On the other hand, we had another student who arrived and revealed to the dorm director that he had ten thousand dollars in cash and a credit card to pay for his education. We documented the amount of his money and locked it up in a safe.

The most difficult issues in educating young people are in the area of morals. There is a constant struggle of dealing with dress (or lack of dress) and sexual encounters. Proverbs 22:6 says, "Train up a child in the way he should go: and when he is old, he will not depart from it." There is a difference between "telling" and "training." We inform students of our standards before they ever arrive for class. These standards are clearly printed in the *Student Handbook* and are meticulously reviewed in student orientation. We tell the students of these standards in chapel and in class. The word "train" means "to hedge in" and can be described as a Texas cowboy fencing in his cattle so they can go in only one direction. The cattle may resist, but the cowboy will get them into the pen. Occasionally, one may escape to ranch lands, but the cowboy will find it in a day or two and get it back into the pen. Like cowboys, personnel at a Christian college must work to guide the students in the right direction. In fact, the first name for Christians before they were called "Christians" was "people of the Way." They were known to follow the way of Christ. Many students come from dysfunctional homes where little to no guidance was given and find "following" to be a difficult concept. Therefore, they need training that is consistent and comprehensive.

Education in the areas of mind, money, and morals need to start early in the home. This education needs to be reinforced with biblical teachings from the church and Christian colleges. If a person does not follow God's way, then he or she will experience vanity—emptiness of life (Phillips Vol.2, 180).

Prayer
"God, I pray that You will place a hedge of protection around every student at Jacksonville College so that they will not stray from Your Word.

Personal Reflection
List the three areas of mind, money, and morals. Think and write ways you personally need to change in order to live by the truth of God's Word.

"Punny"
Q: What is the most slippery country in the world?
A: Greece

Favorite of Jacob Andrew Gardner (grandson of author)
Born May 5, 2005

Plan to Share Today
Plan to share what you learned and what you laughed at with someone today.

Proverbs 23

Wrong Road

Passage
Read Proverbs 23.

Most have experienced the frustration of choosing the wrong road and losing time and patience. History is filled with tragedies about lives that have gone down the wrong path. Proverbs 22-24 are "Thirty Sayings" that follow a pattern used by ancient authors who present differences in the often traveled roads of life (Garrett 193).

Proverbs 23: 1-3 warns to be careful about what you eat, how much you eat, and with whom you eat.

Proverbs 23:4-8 warns of pursuing wealth that ends in disaster.

Proverbs 23:9-12 warns of not listening to fools but rather seeking to be educated.

Proverbs 23:13-25 warns about the dangers of not listening to your parents.

Proverbs 23:26-35 warns about the pitfalls of immorality with prostitutes and drunkenness.

There is a path that leads to life and a path that leads to death. The right path honors parents, pastors, teachers, and mentors of youth (Bailey 143).

The point is do not exclude God or the godly teaching of others from your choices in life. It is a big mistake to travel down the road of life and leave God out of your choices. Mychal Judge served as a Chaplain for the New York Fire Department. He died on 9/11. When they recovered his body, they found on him a prayer. "Lord, take me where You want me to go; Let me meet who You want me to meet; Tell me what You want me to say, and; Keep me out of Your way" (Dykes).

Prayer
"God, thank You for turning on the light of Christ and the light for a desire to learn."

Personal Reflection
Ask yourself, "Why do I want to learn? Is it for head knowledge or for heart-life transformation?"

"Punnies"

Q: How do bears walk around?
A: With bare feet

Q: What kind of pen does a baby prefer?
A: A playpen

Favorites of Lance Curtis Smith (son of author)
Born June 26, 1976

Plan to Share Today

Plan to share what you learned and what you laughed at with someone today.

Proverbs 24
Evil

Passage

Read Proverbs 24.

Solomon said much about evil people. Over sixty times he penned a proverb about evil.

1. How is evil defined?

   In Proverbs 24:1, the Hebrew word for "evil" means "wicked" or a person who destroys that which is good. These people lack a moral compass or standard. During the infamous Watergate investigation, the Judge asked Nixon aide Jeb Magruder, "How could you have done what you did?" I will never forget Magruder's answer. He said, "Judge, somewhere along the way I lost my moral compass." Evil people focus on one direction, and that direction is to do evil.

2. How is evil manifested?

   a. Heart (verse 2)

      Evil begins in the heart. Without the presence of the Holy Spirit in a person's life, evil cannot be restrained. Consequently, the evil person does whatever he or she desires. The heart of the lost person is desperately wicked.

   b. Lips (verse 2)

      Notice that in this verse, the lips of evil people stir up trouble. Do you want to know who is evil? Listen to them speak. Evil people are troublemakers and trouble-talkers.

   c. Mind (verse 8)

      Evil people plan and plot to do evil. John Phillips tells of a conversation he had with a pastor friend who had been a former street gang member in Chicago. The pastor explained that the leaders of the gang were called "gators," a shortened form of the word "instigators." These instigators were the gang leaders who came up with the plan to do evil. The rest of the gang would carry out the plot. This real life example is played out in many television crime shows that seek to uncover the mastermind behind the plot. An evil person has a passion and purpose to mastermind evil (Phillips Vol. 2, 267).

3. How is evil avoided? (verses 1, 19-20)
   Verse 1 says to stay away from evil. Sometimes staying away is hard because the world is full of evil people. Taylor Swift sings a popular song, "Why Ya Gotta Be So Mean?" (I really believe my granddaughter Emma said it first to her brother William). God tells us not to worry about evil people. Don't try to get even with them. Christians should stay focused. Do right when others do wrong.

Prayer
"God, help me do right when evil is all around me."

Personal Reflection
Write out what your response will be when someone wants you to do evil.

"Punny"
Q: Why do bakers work so hard?
A: Because they need the dough

Favorite of Lance Curtis Smith (son of author)
Born June 26, 1976

Plan to Share Today
Plan to share what you learned and what you laughed at with someone today.

Proverbs 25
Conflict

Passage
Read Proverbs 25

Some people believe that King Hezekiah may be the author of Proverbs 25-29. Hezekiah was the 14th king of Judah in 716-686 B.C. He was a good king who restored true worship in Judah by destroying idols and cleaning up the temple. I believe that as a reward for Hezekiah's faithfulness, God allowed Hezekiah's men to find these writings so that they could be included in Proverbs. Though Judah enjoyed spiritual stability and moral order under Hezekiah, the nation experienced major conflict with the country of Assyria. The Bible records 133 cases of conflict. Just as conflict was a part of Hezekiah's day, there is no question that you will have conflict. The question that needs an answer, however, is how you will respond to conflict.

1. Control your temper (verse 8).
   Pick your battles. Some things that are said and done to you need to "roll off your back." Don't be so sensitive. If you are a person with a quick, hot temper, you will experience much conflict. If you are prone to lean that way, you will meet your match; it will be ugly.

2. Control your tongue (verses 9-11).
   When you have conflict, go to the person by yourself, sit down, listen to his or her side, and resolve the matter. Jesus gives this same counsel in Matthew 18. Sadly, most people do not follow that advice. Instead of going to the person with whom they are having conflict, they go tell others.

Many people are quick to resolve an issue through litigation. Today's society is "sue happy." Instead of seeking to resolve conflicts according to Jesus' guidelines, people go to court and let a judge or jury decide. Before you go to court, you need a good cause, a good counselor, and a good credit card. I am not saying Christians should never go to court; sometimes our culture will not allow any other resolution. The biblical way to resolve conflict is with the person with whom you are in conflict.

Prayer
"God, control my tongue today."

Personal Reflection
If you are in conflict with anyone, pray. Then go and talk to that person and agree to pray together until there is a resolution.

"Punnies"
Q: Where do baby trees go to school?
A: At a nursery

Q: Where do worms like to go for dinner?
A: Some place dirt cheap

Favorites of Asheley René Ferguson Smith (daughter-in-law of author)
Born October 30, 1978

Plan to Share Today
Plan to share what you learned and what you laughed at with someone today.

Proverbs 26
Fools

Passage
Read Proverbs 26.

The English word for "fool" comes from the Latin word *follis*, which means "bellows." The term "fool" is used to describe a person with puffed-up cheeks or someone who is full of hot air. In the Hebrew language, there are three different words translated as fool. *Kesyl* is the stupid, dull, stubborn fool. *Ewiyl* is the corrupt fool who is morally perverted and unreasonable. *Nabal* is the fool who is like a stubborn, brutish animal (Wiersbe 90-91).

Solomon gives some warnings and words of wisdom when dealing with fools:

1. Separate (verses 1-2)
   In these verses, Solomon says that snow does not belong in summer and rain has no place at harvest. The fool is not worthy of honor. Do not associate with fools; do not honor a fool with your presence. The best way to react to a fool's folly and foolishness is to tell him or her, "Get away from me."

2. Spare not (verse 3)
   In controlling animals, the master must use a whip and a bridle. A whip spurs him on, and a bridle holds him back. Sometimes animals need to go, and sometimes they need to stop. Solomon warns not to spare the rod of correction when trying to control fools.

3. Speak (verse 4)
   Verse 4 is very clear: "Do not answer a fool according to his folly." You cannot reason with a fool, so do not waste time trying to talk with a fool. At times, you need to tell a fool, "Stop, I'm not going to listen or participate in your foolishness."

Fools do not learn from their mistakes. Like a dog, they return to their own vomit (verse 11). There is no hope for a conceited person who is a fool. The captain of the Titanic refused to listen to the warning about the iceberg, and the ship sank as a result. The sentence of a fool is death.

Prayer
"Lord, help me not to be a fool, unless it is to be a "fool for Jesus."

Personal Reflection
Think of someone you believe is a fool, and compare his or her words and actions to the words and actions of a wise man as described in the Bible.

"Punny"
Q: What did Adam say to his wife the day before Christmas?
A: "It's Christmas, Eve!"

Favorite of Asheley René Ferguson Smith (daughter-in-law of author)
Born October 30, 1978

Plan to Share Today
Plan to share what you learned and what you laughed at with someone today.

Proverbs 27
Accountability

Passage

Read Proverbs 27.

Proverbs 27:17 says, "Iron sharpeneth iron; so a man sharpeneth the countenance of his friend." This proverb speaks of the influence one man can have on another man. Friends learn from each other. This verse stresses the need for good friends who will hold you accountable.

Early in my ministry, a man, large in stature, took time with me. We often ate together and traveled to ministerial meetings together. He opened the Bible and taught me like no seminary professor. When I moved to a small town, I got up early, walked a mile to Whataburger, drank coffee, and visited with another friend. He and I were opposite on several issues, but he was so kind in his rebukes that I valued his friendship. When I became Director of Missions for Dogwood Trails Association, I moved to Jacksonville, Texas. For the first fourteen years, every Wednesday morning at 8:00 you could find me in a corner booth at Dairy Queen with several friends. We had book studies, Bible studies, and long, open debates.

When I worked at the Southern Baptists of Texas Convention office, I was constantly on the go. It seemed impossible to develop friendships, but there was a co-worker who liked me and was also an early riser. Whoever arrived at the office first would make the coffee. We would talk and drink that first cup together before going about our busy day. Currently, on Mondays at noon, I travel to a nearby Italian restaurant and have lunch with several men. Some of these men are preachers and some are professionals in the community. We have become great friends. When you spend time with real friends, you can walk into the room, take one glance at their faces, and their countenances will tell you what they need. Friends need to be accountable to each other.

Certainly your closest friend should be your mate. Between Susan and me, I am usually the first one up. I have my quiet time with Jesus; I make the coffee, and then Susan wanders in. We each sit in our easy chairs and visit as we have those first twelve cups of coffee. These mornings are the sweetest times of life. My advice to any young man is to listen to Solomon in Proverbs 21:19 and do not marry a contentious woman, but marry your best friend who can change your character in a sweet, special way.

Prayer
"God, thank You for friends and thank You for my best friend—my wife."

Personal Reflection
How many friends do you have? Make friends and make time for friends.

"Punnies"
Q: What did the mother buffalo say to her son as he was leaving?
A: "Bison"

Q: What sport comes after nine but before eleven?
A: Ten-nis

Favorites of Logan Curtis Smith (grandson of author)
Born January 9, 2004

Plan to Share Today
Plan to share what you learned and what you laughed at with someone today.

Proverbs 28
Leaders

Passage

Read Proverbs 28

Solomon, as he often does, uses the technique of contrast. In this proverb, he is contrasting evil leaders and righteous leaders.

Within two centuries, northern Israel had nine different dynasties, and civil wars were constantly recurring because of poor leaders who led the nation to be unfaithful to God. In the south, Judah had one dynasty whose rulers tended to be mostly God-fearing kings. A definite connection exists between a nation's morality, political turmoil, and, ultimately, military defeat. American citizens need to understand this connection before it is too late.

What are the characteristics of a good leader?

1. Respects God
   Notice the contrast and warning in Verse 5—"Evil men understand not judgment: but they that seek the Lord understand all things." Leaders who lead from a humanistic belief deny God and have no absolutes. Good leaders believe in God and base their approach to life on God's Word.

2. Rules justly
   Verse 13—"He that covereth his sins shall not prosper: but whoso confesseth and forsaketh them shall have mercy."

3. Reaches out to the needy
   Verse 27—"He that giveth unto the poor shall not lack: but he that hideth his eyes shall have many a curse."

A leader is concerned about the needs of other people and takes necessary steps to relieve distress and bring comfort to those who are hurting. John D. Rockefeller became the world's first billionaire. By age 53, he was making one million dollars a week, was the richest man in the world, and, as some might say, looked like death warmed over. He had contracted a disease that caused him to lose all of his hair, and he could eat nothing but crackers and milk. He started giving away money to numerous needs. From his retirement in 1896 until his death in 1937, he gave away three times as much money as he had made. He regained his health and lived to be 97 years old (Phillips Vol.2, 441).

God-fearing leaders are desperately needed in all areas of society: community organizations, families, churches, and nations. Ungodly rulers can be disastrous.

Prayer
"God, I pray You raise up God-fearing leaders."

Personal Reflection
Make a list that compares the characteristics of a good leader with those of a bad leader.

"Punny"
Q: What did the baby corn say to the mommy corn?
A: "Where is Pop-corn?"

Favorite of Logan Curtis Smith (grandson of author)
Born January 9, 2004

Plan to Share Today
Plan to share what you learned and what you laughed at with someone today.

Proverbs 29
Vision

Passage

Read Proverbs 29

Proverbs 29:18, "Where there is no vision, the people perish: he that keepeth the law, happy is he."

1. Vision—The Hebrew word for "vision" is also translated as "revelation."
2. People perish—"People perish" can also be translated as "unrestrained."
3. But he that keepeth the law—This phrase describes the person who knows and obeys God's Word.
4. Happy is he—"He" is a person who is completely fulfilled.

Jacksonville College is unique because it is the only two-year, faith-based college left in the state of Texas. When its founders met, their vision was to start a Christian college in East Texas. Their vision became a reality in 1899 with the founding of Jacksonville College. Today, JC continues to cast a vision for its students. Our vision is reflected in our mission statement: "Jacksonville College exists to provide a quality education from a biblical worldview that challenges minds, transforms lives, and equips students for servant leadership and lifelong learning."

Every semester at Jacksonville College, we have numerous students who come for various reasons. Some students enroll to gain independence from their parents; some come seeking the college social life; some students enroll to follow the dream of being in professional sports; others come to seriously pursue a career. While some may know what field they wish to pursue, many do not have a declared major.

Jacksonville College is a good place for all of these students. JC offers the Texas Core Curriculum, which requires 60 hours of basic liberal arts courses. Every Texas college student is required to take the same mathematics, science, English, and history courses. In addition, students at JC are required to take 6 hours of religion and attend weekly chapel services. As a liberal arts college, JC offers each student time to discover his or her major field of study.

A person with no revelation, direction, or purpose in life will continue to chase one pursuit after another, but a person who seeks to listen to God's word will be fulfilled. Every semester, I see students who have a heart for God, who read and study His Word, and pray to discover God's purpose for their lives. These students are more confident, become better students in all disciplines, and seek to serve God and their fellow man.

Prayer
"God, thank You for giving purpose, meaning, and direction in life."

Personal Reflection
Write out your personal vision or mission statement.

"Punnies"
Q: Where do you take a sick puppy?
A: To the dog-tor

Q: How do you catch a runaway computer?
A: With an inter-net

Favorites of Landon Cole Smith (grandson of author)
Born November 7, 2006

Plan to Share Today
Plan to share what you learned and what you laughed at with someone today.

Proverbs 30
Bucket List

Passage

Read Proverbs 30.

Proverbs 30:18-19, "There be three things which are too wonderful for me, yea, four which I know not: The way of an eagle in the air; the way of a serpent upon a rock; the way of a ship in the midst of the sea; and the way of a man with a maid."

After the movie *The Bucket List* came out, people started using the term "bucket list" to refer to activities they would like to do or places they would like to visit before they died or "kicked the bucket." In Proverbs 30, Solomon gives several lists, but my focus will be on the list in verses 18-19. In this list, Solomon says that there are four things too wonderful for him to understand. The late Dr. W.A. Criswell, the pastor at First Baptist Church in Dallas for over 50 years, wrote a book called *The Scarlet Thread through the Bible.* According to Criswell, the key to interpreting the Bible is to understand how Christ, the scarlet thread, is revealed in every book from Genesis to Revelation. Therefore, the key to understanding Solomon's list is understanding how Christ is revealed in the four things that are too wonderful for Solomon to understand. With this in mind, look at how John Phillips, author of *Exploring Proverbs,* explains how Solomon reveals Christ in this list:

1. Eagle—Eagles build nests higher than the flight capabilities of other birds. Their vision is eight times greater than man's vision. The eagle can fly so high that you cannot see the eagle, but the eagle can see you. Christ is God, and His home is heaven. He looked down, saw the sin of man, and came down to Earth as a man—Jesus.

2. Snake—The blood temperature of a snake is one degree lower than the air, so as the air gets colder, the snake slows down. As the sun shines and the air is warmed, the snake moves itself out onto warm rocks. In this example, Christ is NOT compared to the snake but to the sun that shines and warms the air. As Christ, the sun, begins to shine, Satan always tries to move into action and steal His glory.

71

3. Ship—In biblical times, ships were dependent on the sky and wind. The captains of ships would look to the sky to see if the conditions were right for sailing. The ships were powered by the wind. Jesus was conceived by the Holy Spirit (symbolized by the wind) and controlled by the Spirit. Jesus, while on this earth, was a perfect man who looked to God in what he should do ("not my will but Thine"). Jesus never did anything apart from the Spirit of God.

4. Woman—On the surface, you would think a man with one thousand wives would understand the way with a maid. But Solomon confessed even after being married to one thousand women that he did not understand them and that they were a mystery. In the New Testament, the church is given the feminine identity of the bride of Christ, and He is coming back one day for His church. Christ loved the church and gave Himself for his bride. God's great love for mankind may seem to be a mystery, but that love brought Him to this earth and caused Him to die for you. Love is the way of Christ. Like Solomon's inability to understand the way of a man with a maid, Christ and His love for His church is too wonderful for humanity to fully understand. Just bow down and praise Him (Phillips Vol. 2, 565 outline).

Prayer
"God, besides You there is none other. You alone are worthy to be praised. God, thank You for a love that gave us Jesus, who loved me and redeemed me."

Personal Reflection
List some things in your life that Christ has done for you that are too wonderful to understand but clearly reveal the mystery of God's love.

"Punny"
Q: What do cats call mice on a skateboard?
A: Meals on wheels

Favorite of Landon Cole Smith (grandson of author)
Born November 7, 2006

Plan to Share Today
Plan to share what you learned and what you laughed at with someone today.

Proverbs 31
Wisdom from a Mother

Passage

Read Proverbs 31.

Proverbs begins with words of wisdom from a father (1:8) and ends with words of wisdom from a mother (31:1-2). Concerning the identity of King Lemuel, the Talmud, central text of Rabbinic Judaism, says that "Lemuel" was just another name for Solomon. As to the identity of Solomon's mother, she was Bathsheba. This devotional concerns the wisdom that Bathsheba imparts to Solomon.

In Proverbs 31:10-31, Solomon takes the advice of his mother and uses the twenty-two letters of the Hebrew alphabet to form an acrostic that describes the characteristics of a virtuous woman. In the following, please permit me to use my wife, Susan, as an example.

1. Special (verses 11-12, 27-29)
   Susan is a very special woman because she loves her husband (me) and her children as much or more than any other woman could. Not being critical but observational, women today seek careers, fame, honor, and recognition. Susan, first and foremost, sought to love and care for her family. Today, our children—Martha and Lance—are who they are largely because of Susan.

2. Supportive (verses 13-20)
   Soon after we were married, I informed Susan that we were going to Illinois to start a church. She graciously followed me. We lived in an unairconditioned, 8 x 15 foot trailer that was located in a cornfield. Over the years, she worked alongside me and followed me from one ministry place to another. I could not have asked for better support from her.

3. Stunning (verses 21-27)
   When I say stunning, I do not mean this term in a worldly way. Susan never dressed or acted in an ungodly fashion but clothed herself like the virtuous woman with honor and strength. She cared for her body as a temple of God, and she honored me by always being attractively dressed. She is a beautiful, virtuous woman, the most stunning woman I've ever seen. My heart still skips a beat when I look at her.

4. Spiritual (verses 28-31)

    Susan gets up early. We usually drink a pot of coffee together and go over the day's activities. She prepares my breakfast, and after I leave for the day, she goes to her special place with a hymn book and Bible and has her quiet time. She always seeks God. Susan was saved at the early age of eight at the foot of her mother. Her love for God is the foundation for all of her other characteristics. Susan is special, and I am blessed to have her as my wife.

Prayer

"God, thank You for the blessing of my wife and for the years we've spent together."

Personal Reflection

If you are married, tell your wife how much you love her and take her out to eat. If you are not married, identify a virtuous woman you can honor in some special way.

"Punny"

Q: Why are fish afraid to play volleyball?
A: They might get caught in the net.

Favorite of Susan Claire Springer Smith (wife of author)
Born May 21, 1950

Plan to Share Today

Plan to share what you learned and what you laughed at with someone today.

CONTRIBUTIONS

I have a procedure that I like to follow when I study God's Word. First, I pray and then read the passage in several different translations. Next, I use inductive Bible study methods. These methods usually consist of asking and answering a series of who, what, when, where, and why questions for each passage. Finally, I consult my friends. My friends are the commentaries written by various authors. I've also gained respect for the authors from reading their works or from hearing them speak. Through my inductive study, I am either confirmed in what I believe or convicted that I need to study more. I try to always give credit when I use the works of others. Sometimes I quote others, and sometimes they trigger a thought in me that I try to make my own. My friends in studying Proverbs are:

Bailey, Boyd. *Through Proverbs*. Eugene: Harvest House, 2015. Print.

Dykes, David. "9/11—Five Years Later: Finding Hope for Your Future." Green Acres Baptist Church, Tyler, TX. 10 Sept. 2006. Sermon.

Garrett, Duane, A. *The New American Commentary*. Vol. 14. Nashville: B&H Publishers, 1993. Print.

Laird, Douglas L. *Why Worry*. Litchfield Park, AZ: Christian Stewardship Ministries, 1993. Print.

Phillips, John. *Exploring Proverbs: An Expository Commentary*. Vol. 1. Grand Rapids: Kregel, 1995. Print.

Phillips, John. *Exploring Proverbs: An Expository Commentary*. Vol. 2. Grand Rapids: Kregel, 1996. Print.

Wiersbe, Warren W. *Be Skillful*. Colorado Springs: Cook, 1995. Print.

I would like to acknowledge the great contribution of my proofreaders, Dr. David Heflin, Vanita Pettey, and Marolyn Welch.

I want to thank God for my family and the many moments of tears and laughter we have experienced together. These priceless experiences make Proverbs so true to life for me.

Obituary and Eulogy for James Owen Springer

By Mike Smith

In Psalm 121, the Traveler Psalm, and Psalm 23, God's Word gives us great help for occasions such as the death of a loved one. We are always saddened when death invades a family circle. While this is a tender hour, this is in no way an hour of tragedy. We are here to honor our Lord and Savior in His work and to celebrate the life and home-going of James Owen Springer.

James Owen Springer was born December 7, 1920, in Terrell, Texas. James graduated from Terrell High School in 1937. He was also a graduate of Southern Methodist University School of Banking. He served with honor in World War II in the Army Air Corps and received three medals: the Distinguished Flying Cross, the Air Medal with Oak Leaf Cluster, and the Asiatic Pacific Campaign Medal with Five Bronze Stars. James worked at American National Bank of Terrell for forty-four years and retired as Senior Vice-President. He was active in the Terrell community, serving as treasurer for several civic organizations such as the Red Cross and the Salvation Army. He was an active member of the First Baptist Church of Terrell, serving as a Sunday School teacher, a deacon, and a member of numerous committees.

James was preceded in death by his parents, James Oliver Springer and Lottie Myrtle Roberts Springer; two sisters, Mary Helen, who died at age three, and Getta Fern Davis; one son, James Owen, who died at birth; and one son-in-law, Joe Chambers. Also preceding him in death was his beloved wife of seventy-one years, Emily Nell Henderson Springer. He joined her in heaven on Thursday, January 28, 2016.

James is survived by two daughters, Carol Chambers of Spring, Texas, and Susan Smith and husband Mike of Jacksonville, Texas; five grandchildren, Cyndi Hudson and husband Bob of Senatobia, Mississippi; Mason Rollins of The Woodlands, Texas; Allison Combrink and husband Lance of The Woodlands, Texas; Elaine Gardner and husband James of West Monroe, Louisiana, and Lance Smith and wife Asheley of Flint, Texas; ten great-grandchildren, Adam Hudson of Spring, Texas; Ross Hudson of Senatobia,

Mississippi; Mason, Jack, and Alexa Combrink of The Woodlands, Texas; William, Emma, and Jacob Gardner of West Monroe, Louisiana, and Logan and Landen Smith of Flint, Texas; one sister-in-law, Evalyn Crouch and husband James of Terrell, Texas; one brother-in-law, John Vance of Rockwall, Texas; nephews, Keith Crouch and wife Sarah, and Paul Crouch and wife Phyllis; nieces, Teresa Norvell and husband Monty, and Jan Crawford and husband Pat; and a host of friends.

James would say, "Most of my friends are dead," but the crowd here today is evidence that this is not the case. He was loved by many.

Every morning, James called Susan and wanted to know where Susan and I were going to be on Sunday. He knew that I had been preaching out of 2 Corinthians for the last several weeks, and those of us who loved James can take comfort in Paul's words in 2 Corinthians 5:8-21 (KJV):

> [8]We are confident, I say, and willing rather to be absent from the body, and to be present with the Lord. [9]Wherefore we labour, that, whether present or absent, we may be accepted of him. [10]For we must all appear before the judgment seat of Christ; that every one may receive the things done in his body, according to that he hath done, whether it be good or bad. [11]Knowing therefore the terror of the Lord, we persuade men; but we are made manifest unto God; and I trust also are made manifest in your consciences. [12]For we commend not ourselves again unto you, but give you occasion to glory on our behalf, that ye may have somewhat to answer them which glory in appearance, and not in heart. [13]For whether we be beside ourselves, it is to God: or whether we be sober, it is for your cause. [14]For the love of Christ constraineth us; because we thus judge, that if one died for all, then were all dead: [15]And that he died for all, that they which live should not henceforth live unto themselves, but unto him which died for them, and rose again. [16]Wherefore henceforth know we no man after the flesh: yea, though we have known Christ after the flesh, yet now henceforth know we him no more. [17]Therefore if any man be in Christ, he is a new creature: old things are passed away; behold, all things are become new. [18]And all things are of God, who hath reconciled us to himself by Jesus Christ, and hath given to us the ministry of reconciliation; [19]To wit, that God was in Christ,

reconciling the world unto himself, not imputing their trespasses unto them; and hath committed unto us the word of reconciliation. [20]Now then we are ambassadors for Christ, as though God did beseech you by us: we pray you in Christ's stead, be ye reconciled to God. [21]For he hath made him to be sin for us, who knew no sin; that we might be made the righteousness of God in him.

Tom Brokaw referred to those born in 1914-1929 as the "Greatest Generation." In the 1940s, there were 16 million of this generation in World War II. Today, there are less than 600,000 of this generation left. Each day, 430 of this generation die—that is one person every three seconds. James Springer was one of the Greatest Generation. Many characteristics are worth noting about this generation: they lived during the Great Depression; they fought in the Big One of World War II, and they came home and built a great nation. A great nation is made of great men, and James Springer was a great man who loved his family, lived his faith, and looked forward for his future home in heaven.

<u>Family</u>

James was born on December 7, 1920. Dr. Neely delivered the baby at 2:00 a.m. in the Springer's home. James's father owned Hi-Lo Grocery at the corner of Blanch and High. One characteristic of the "Greatest Generation" is their strong work ethic. James's first job was working at Hi-Lo. It was the first of drive-in groceries. James said that people would drive up and holler, "I want 10¢ of cheese and crackers and a slice of bologna." Either James or his Uncle Lowrie would take the groceries out to the car. Since many people didn't have a car, customers could also call in their orders, and James and his Uncle Lowrie would deliver the groceries to them. At 15 years old, James got a job at Self Bakery and worked on Saturdays. He got up at 3:00 a.m. and delivered bread to various stores and cafes in Terrell. Later that day, he went back and collected 6¢ a loaf.

In high school, James played sports. In football, he was a halfback. Today, much is said about head injuries to football players, but James and his teammates played without helmets. He said the first game he ever played was the first time he had ever seen football because he didn't have a television. In baseball, he played centerfield. In track, he ran 440 and won the Kaufman County meet. He would have gone to State, but he hurt his knee.

The day after he graduated Terrell High School, he went to B&J Sales, bought a hoe, and got a job from Mr. Ayers in Friendship community where he chopped cotton for $1 a day. James said that in football he never had a water break, so he was use to going without water, which prepared him for chopping cotton. He said that Mr. Ayer had a lot of hands working for him, and he brought one bucket of water that had only one dipper. James said he watched those old hands dip snuff, saw the snuff run down the sides of their faces, and then saw them drink out of the dipper. He said that he could not drink after them, so he would go all day without water.

Mr. Gill of American National Bank had been watching James in the community. He sent word for James to come and see him, and on July 26, 1939, James started working at American National Bank six days a week from 7:30 a.m. to 6:00 p.m. for $50 a month. He figured the price of cotton on a Burroughs posting machine. He worked his way up the ranks in the bank and retired as Senior Vice President. James valued the relationship he had with Mr. Gill and the Hulsey family.

James and Emily Henderson were in Terrell High School together and attended FBC Terrell. When James went off to the Army, they corresponded through letters. James got a seven-day pass and came home to Terrell, and he and Emily decided to get married. On May 22, 1943, with one day of preparation, the couple went to Kaufman for a license, got flowers, told their parents about their plans, and went to the preacher's house where Bro. Doss married them at 4:00 p.m. After they got married, they went to Dallas for a short honeymoon and were separated for the next year and a half while James served in the Army.

After being overseas, James came back to Ft. Wayne, Indiana, where Emily joined him; then they moved to West Monroe, Louisiana. They were on the freedom bridge in Monroe when the war ended. After his honorable discharge, James and Emily came to Terrell and both worked and built a family together. Emily worked at Southwestern Bell as an operator, and James worked at American National Bank. Carol and Susan were born during this time.

Family, work, and church were their life. James loved his family and enjoyed knowing what they were doing. Sometimes the grandkids spent the night. Emily would try to get them to sleep, and James would come in and pretend to be a monster and wake them up. At times, Emily thought that James was too hard or stern with the children. Tom Brokaw's mother tells of a man in the "Greatest Generation" era who was their neighbor. The man was complaining about a group of rowdy 17-year-olds in the neighborhood who were making a lot of noise the previous night. Mrs. Brokaw tried to help her neighbors and said, "They are just 17, what were *you* doing at 17?" The man looked her in the eye and said, "When I was 17, I landed on the Guadalcanal and killed Japanese soldiers." This explains some of the seriousness and lack of patience of the "Greatest Generation" with the younger generation.

Psalm 37:23 says, "The steps of a good man are ordered by the Lord." James would tell you the hand of God was upon his life.

Faith

James grew up in FBC Terrell under the very biblical, conservative preaching of Bro. Doss. James was a Sunday School teacher. He had many Bibles, including a 1939 C.I. Scofield Bible. When I went to ask James for Susan's hand in marriage, I was very nervous. James asked me what kind of Bible I used. When I told him a red-letter Scofield Bible, he seemed to give his approval of me. He loved God's Word, and he was a man of prayer. In this Bible, he listed the names of each of the members of his Sunday School class, and he prayed faithfully for all of them. In 2003, he taught a class of 28 members, and next to their names he had written the death dates of 13 of those members.

James had a realistic view of life and death and knew that he needed God's protection. There are three stories James shared with me from the war that confirmed God protected him:

1. After basic training, James wanted to go with his friend to gunner school, but when a medical exam revealed James had high blood pressure, his group went on and James was sent to radio school. Later, he found out that nearly everyone in his training group was killed in the early battles of war. He said that Emily and Grandmother D's prayers caused his blood pressure to rise.

2. He was with the 69th Troop 433 cargo plane in the Pacific stationed in New Guinea. They flew to Sydney, Australia, then flew over the combat zone to drop supplies to the troops. One day when they were already in the plane to take off, Japanese fighters attacked. They jumped out of the plane and hid in tall grass. James said a Japanese fighter pilot got so low to shoot that he saw the whites of the eyes of the pilot. James believed he lived to tell the story because God spared him.

3. On one mission, his team loaded up and began their flight over Stanley Mountain. This forced them to climb 10,000 feet without oxygen. The carburetor froze; the plane went into a tail spin, and the pilot Lt. Cole howled, "Bail out!" James said he didn't have a parachute. He fell on the floor of the plane and prayed because he knew they were going to die. Another crewman, Gig-e-o, jumped into the pilot seat and went to work. Within 1,000 feet of crashing, the plane leveled out. Later, a mechanic said there was no way they should be alive—the carburetor was frozen. James said, "God reached down and pulled the plane up."

I was James and Emily's pastor for a time. After retirement, James enjoyed going on mission trips with me. On one trip to Minnesota, I asked James if he would teach the laymen about finance/stewardship while I taught the pastors on preaching. We had a good group. After the session one night, James came to me and said, "Mike, you asked me to teach on finances, and not one man in my group has a job. They are all on welfare. I believe we need to change the topic." He enjoyed telling me that story.

Another time, James and my dad drove a motor home for 24 straight hours to Minnesota, and four of us preachers played the game of 42 all the way. When we got to Minnesota, it was 50°F below zero. The motor home froze, and we had cases of Coke that froze and popped all night while we slept in the motor home. I woke up at 4:00 a.m. James was outside doing exercises to keep from freezing while he waited for one of the preachers to wake up so he could go back inside. James loved telling others what he told preacher Kenneth Simmons, a missionary in Minnesota, "Kenneth, if I left anything here, you sell it and keep the money 'cause I'm never coming back to this frozen-over swamp."

Faith and family were James's life, but James also had many hobbies and other interests. He was an avid reader and a student of the Civil War. He collected guns and knives, reloaded ammunition, was a wood carver, and enjoyed photography. He traveled to every county in Texas and shot pictures of courthouses. He also shot pictures of good restaurants, like Bobcat Bites in Santa Fe, Country Tavern in Kilgore, and The Shed in Edom. He would take pictures of unusual road signs like "Duck Crossing" and "Cattle Motel." He enjoyed camping; he started with a canvas tent, moved to a pick-up shell, then moved to a camper or trailer. He enjoyed farming and cows. He and my son, Lance, had a cattle business and would talk about fixing fences. He enjoyed genealogy and going to old cemeteries. In the town of Priddy, he asked a man if he could go across his land to an old cemetery. He crossed the fence, but Emily could not climb over, so he had to pick up Emily to get her over the fence. He got a good laugh out of it. He enjoyed music and played the harmonica. Susan often found him in his chair playing the harmonica. He said to her, "See, I can entertain myself." In a recent hospital visit, a pastor friend of mine was in the same hospital as James. My friend said he was depressed and hurting and then heard beautiful singing. He walked down the hall and ended up talking to James. After being with James, he left encouraged and filled with joy.

Future

James did not worry about the future. He settled the matter as a young boy and trusted Jesus as Savior. On Monday night, the week of his death, I went to the emergency room in Jacksonville and sat with him. The doctors said that they needed to transport him to Tyler. I did not really think very seriously of this because he had been in the hospital before and recovered. I really thought James would live to be 100 years old. We used to joke that at 100 we would put his picture on a Smucker's jar of jelly to air on NBC. Carol came the next day and stayed with him, then Susan arrived on Wednesday. James was told the cancer had spread and hospice needed to be called. Carol and Susan had a special time with their dad. The next morning James died.

When he learned about his approaching death, James did not fret or lose control. He knew his future was okay because of Jesus. He had a strong faith in Jesus and shared his faith in his Sunday School class, at the bank, and on mission trips. The night before he died, he shared with the nurse that he was a

Christian and had put his trust in Jesus. Following is the letter from his Army friend, Schade:

July 11, 2012

James,

This is an important NOTE to you:

For a long time I've meant to tell you how much you've influenced me at the great meaning of God and His Son, Jesus Christ in my life. He's guided me and has given me direction, strength, love, and comfort to guide me thru this Life on Earth in hopes of reaching the "Promise Land."

I look to our meeting in Heaven!

Sincerely,

Billy Schade, of the old 69th Squadron of the 433rd T.C. Group WWII

James was a very generous man who shared with others the wealth with which God had blessed him. He shared with Southwestern Seminary (was a founding member of the President's Club), Dallas Baptist University, Jacksonville College, NRA, Williamsburg, and Indian School. God had given him much, and he shared. I tried to get him to stop giving to the seminary and give it all to Jacksonville College, but he gave to both. When I related this to the congregation, Travis Trawick from Southwestern Seminary was present and Paige Patterson had sent white roses.

James was ready for the future. Are you? In his Bible he had marked the Roman Road.

1. Romans 3:23, "For all have sinned, and come short of the glory of God."
2. Romans 6:23, "For the wages of sin is death; but the gift of God is eternal life through Jesus Christ our Lord."
3. Romans 10:9-10, "That if thou shalt confess with thy mouth the Lord Jesus, and shalt believe in thine heart that God hath raised him from the dead, thou shalt be saved. For with the heart man

believeth unto righteousness; and with the mouth confession is made unto salvation."

James was secure in his future because he asked Jesus into his life. Have you trusted Jesus? If not, James would want you to do so before it is too late.

Visit www.IslandEntertainmentMedia.com for more

information on getting your book published, or to

order individual volumes.

Made in the USA
Charleston, SC
15 September 2016